THE MAGIC OF BOLLYWOOD AND ACCOUNTING

A CINEMATIC JOURNEY THROUGH FINANCIAL STATEMENTS

DEVANG NIRANJAN TRIVEDI

Copyright © Devang Niranjan Trivedi
All Rights Reserved.

This book has been self-published with all reasonable efforts taken to make the material error-free by the author. No part of this book shall be used, reproduced in any manner whatsoever without written permission from the author, except in the case of brief quotations embodied in critical articles and reviews.

The Author of this book is solely responsible and liable for its content including but not limited to the views, representations, descriptions, statements, information, opinions and references ["Content"]. The Content of this book shall not constitute or be construed or deemed to reflect the opinion or expression of the Publisher or Editor. Neither the Publisher nor Editor endorse or approve the Content of this book or guarantee the reliability, accuracy or completeness of the Content published herein and do not make any representations or warranties of any kind, express or implied, including but not limited to the implied warranties of merchantability, fitness for a particular purpose. The Publisher and Editor shall not be liable whatsoever for any errors, omissions, whether such errors or omissions result from negligence, accident, or any other cause or claims for loss or damages of any kind, including without limitation, indirect or consequential loss or damage arising out of use, inability to use, or about the reliability, accuracy or sufficiency of the information contained in this book.

Made with ♥ on the Notion Press Platform
www.notionpress.com

Contents

Introduction

The Magic of Bollywood and Accounting

Bollywood, often considered the heart and soul of Indian cinema, is a vivid tapestry woven with drama, emotion, music, and vibrant storytelling. Its appeal lies in its ability to captivate audiences through a seamless blend of creativity and meticulous execution. Behind every successful Bollywood film is a meticulous structure—an elaborate script, a visionary director, and a talented cast—all coming together to create a cinematic masterpiece. Similarly, accounting, while seemingly a world apart, shares a striking resemblance with filmmaking in its complexity, precision, and the artistry required to tell a compelling story.

Bollywood: A Symphony of Creativity and Precision

In the realm of Bollywood, the journey of creating a film is akin to crafting a beautiful symphony. Each element, from the initial concept to the final cut, must be meticulously orchestrated to ensure harmony and coherence.

1. The Script: The Foundation of the Story

The script is the blueprint of any Bollywood film, much like accounting principles are the foundation of financial reporting. A good script outlines the plot, defines characters, and sets the tone for the entire movie. It acts as a guide for the director, actors, and crew, ensuring that every scene contributes to the overarching narrative.

Similarly, accounting principles like Generally Accepted Accounting Principles (GAAP) and International Financial Reporting Standards (IFRS) provide a structured framework for preparing and presenting financial statements. These principles ensure that financial information is reported consistently, transparently, and accurately, allowing stakeholders to make informed decisions.

1. The Director: The Visionary Leader

In filmmaking, the director is the visionary who transforms the script into a visual and emotional experience. The director's role involves making crucial decisions about the portrayal of characters, the execution of scenes, and the overall tone of the film. The director's vision is crucial for translating the script into a compelling narrative. In accounting, the accountant plays a similar role. Accountants are responsible for ensuring that every financial transaction is recorded correctly and that the financial statements accurately reflect the company's financial position. Just as a director ensures that each scene aligns with the script, an accountant ensures that financial transactions are recorded and reported according to established principles.

3. The Cast: The Key Players

In Bollywood, the cast comprises the lead actors, supporting characters, and extras, each playing a vital role in the film's success. The chemistry and performance of the cast are critical in bringing the script to life. In accounting, the cast of financial statements includes assets, liabilities, and equity. Assets are the resources owned by the company, liabilities represent its obligations, and equity reflects the owners' residual interest in the company. Each component plays a crucial role in the financial story, just as each actor contributes to the overall film narrative.

4. Scenes: The Building Blocks

Scenes are the building blocks of a film, each contributing to the development of the plot and the growth of characters. Every scene adds depth, emotion, and progression to the story. Similarly, financial transactions are the building blocks of accounting. Each transaction—whether it's a sale, a purchase, or an investment—affects the company's financial position. Accurate recording and reporting of these transactions are essential for constructing a clear and accurate financial picture, much like how each scene is essential for telling a cohesive story.

5. The Film Reel: The Comprehensive Record

In filmmaking, the film reel holds all the recorded scenes in sequence. It provides a comprehensive record of the entire film, ensuring that each scene is included and in the correct order. In accounting, the ledger serves a similar purpose. It records all financial transactions in detail, ensuring that every entry is accounted for and that the financial records are accurate and up-to-date. The ledger, like the film reel, is crucial for producing the final financial statements.

6. Editing: Refining the Final Product

Editing is a crucial phase in filmmaking, where the raw footage is refined, and the final product is polished. The editor's job is to ensure continuity, fix errors, and enhance the overall quality of the film. In accounting, adjusting entries serve a similar function. They are made at the end of an accounting period to update the accounts and ensure that financial statements reflect the true economic condition of the company. Just as editing ensures the film is ready for its premiere, adjusting entries ensure that the financial statements are accurate and complete.

7.   The Premiere: The Grand Reveal

The premiere of a film is the moment when the movie is unveiled to the audience. It is the culmination of months or even years of hard work and creativity. Similarly, the financial statements are the grand reveal of the company's financial performance and position. These statements provide a snapshot of the company's financial health and are presented to stakeholders, including investors, creditors, and regulators. Just as the success of a film premiere depends on the quality of the film, the effectiveness of financial statements depends on the accuracy and completeness of the financial reporting.

8.   The Reviews: The Final Assessment

After a film premieres, it is often reviewed by critics and audiences. These reviews assess the film's quality, adherence to standards, and overall impact. In accounting, audits serve a similar purpose. Audits are independent examinations of financial statements to ensure they are accurate and comply with relevant accounting principles.

A clean audit report can enhance a company's credibility and trustworthiness, much like positive reviews can boost a film's success.

Accounting: The Art and Science of Financial Storytelling

Accounting, like Bollywood filmmaking, is both an art and a science. It combines technical skills with creativity to tell the financial story of a business. The principles and practices of accounting are designed to ensure accuracy, consistency, and transparency in financial reporting. Just as a Bollywood film needs a well-crafted script, a skilled director, and a talented cast to succeed, financial reporting requires sound principles, skilled accountants, and accurate records.

In this book, we will explore how Bollywood themes can be used to demystify complex accounting concepts. By drawing parallels between filmmaking and accounting, we aim to make these concepts more relatable and engaging. Each chapter will delve into a specific accounting principle or practice, using Bollywood-inspired examples and dialogues to illustrate how these elements come together to tell the financial story of a business.

From understanding the foundational principles of accounting to exploring the role of accountants, financial transactions, and financial statements, this book will guide you through the world of accounting with a cinematic twist. By the end of this journey, you will have a deeper appreciation for the artistry and precision involved in both Bollywood filmmaking and financial reporting.

Welcome to a unique exploration of accounting through the lens of Bollywood, where financial principles meet cinematic storytelling to create a compelling narrative of business finance.

About Author

Devang N. Trivedi is a seasoned professional with over 30 years of experience in the fields of accounting and finance. His extensive career spans a wide range of roles, including financial analysis, accounting management, and strategic planning. Throughout his career, Devang has been recognized for his profound expertise, meticulous attention to detail, and innovative approach to financial problem-solving.

Devang's journey in the financial world has been marked by a deep commitment to excellence and a passion for demystifying complex accounting concepts. His experience has not only honed his technical skills but also instilled in him a profound understanding of how financial principles apply in various business contexts.

Outside of his professional life, Devang has a longstanding love for cinema, particularly Bollywood films. This passion for movies has been a significant influence on his approach to teaching and writing. He has always been fascinated by how films use storytelling techniques to captivate and educate audiences, and he has drawn inspiration from this art form to make accounting concepts more accessible and engaging.

Motivated by a desire to bridge the gap between complex accounting principles and students who may struggle with understanding these concepts, Devang embarked on a unique project. He recognized that traditional methods of teaching accounting often fall short in making the subject engaging and relatable. To address this challenge, he combined his two passions—accounting and cinema—into an innovative educational approach.

Devang's book, *"The Magic of Bollywood and Accounting,"* is a reflection of his belief that learning can be both informative and entertaining. By drawing analogies between Bollywood filmmaking and accounting principles, Devang aims to simplify financial concepts and make them relatable to students who may be new to the subject. His approach uses familiar elements from Bollywood to explain complex accounting topics, making the learning process more enjoyable and memorable.

In this book, Devang skilfully blends his extensive knowledge of accounting with his love for cinema, creating a unique learning experience. Each chapter is crafted to mirror the various aspects of filmmaking—from the script and the director to the cast and the plot—drawing parallels to accounting principles and practices. This creative approach not only helps demystify accounting for beginners but also engages them in a way that traditional methods may not.

Devang N. Trivedi's dedication to making accounting accessible and his innovative use of cinematic analogies are a testament to his commitment to education and his passion for both his profession and his hobbies. Through this book, he aspires to inspire students, enhance their understanding of accounting, and ignite a lifelong interest in the financial world.

CHAPTER ONE

The Script - Accounting Principles

1.1 Introduction

"Bade bade deshon mein aisi choti choti baatein hoti rehti hain, Senorita." – Dilwale Dulhania Le Jayenge

In the world of accounting, "bade bade companies mein, aise accounting principles hoti rehti hain!" Just like how a movie's script keeps the story in line, accounting principles like GAAP and IFRS ensure that every financial statement is prepared and reported consistently, leaving no room for "choti choti galtiyan" (small mistakes).

In the vibrant world of Bollywood, the script is the very soul of a film. It outlines the plot, shapes the characters, and provides direction, setting the stage for the entire cinematic experience. Without a solid script, even the most talented actors and the most visionary directors would be left adrift, lacking coherence and purpose. Similarly, in the realm of accounting, principles play a crucial role in shaping how financial transactions are recorded and reported. These principles ensure consistency, accuracy, and transparency, allowing stakeholders to make informed decisions based on reliable financial information. This chapter explores the foundational principles of accounting, drawing parallels between the script of a film and the guiding rules of financial reporting.

1.2 GAAP (Generally Accepted Accounting Principles)

Definition

Generally Accepted Accounting Principles (GAAP) is a comprehensive set of rules and standards used primarily in the United States to prepare and present financial statements. These principles are designed to ensure that financial reporting is consistent, transparent, and comparable across different organizations. GAAP encompasses a wide range of guidelines, including how transactions should be recorded, how financial statements should be presented, and how to handle complex financial scenarios.

Key Aspects of GAAP

1. **Consistency**: GAAP requires that financial statements be prepared consistently from one period to the next. This consistency allows stakeholders to compare financial information over time, understanding how a company's financial position and performance have changed.

2. **Relevance**: Financial statements must provide relevant information that is useful for decision-making. This means that the information should be timely, and it should have the ability to influence the decisions of users.

3. **Reliability**: The information presented in financial statements must be accurate and verifiable. Reliable information ensures that users can trust the financial

reports and make informed decisions based on them.

4. **Comparability**: GAAP ensures that financial statements can be compared across different companies. This comparability is crucial for investors and analysts who need to evaluate the performance of different organizations.

Example

Imagine the script of the Bollywood classic *Kabhi Khushi Kabhie Gham* (K3G). This film, with its intricate family drama and multiple storylines, relies on a well-crafted script to ensure that the narrative unfolds logically and coherently. Just as the script guides the actors and directors to maintain consistency and flow in the story, GAAP provides a structured framework for preparing financial statements. In *Kabhi Khushi Kabhie Gham*, the script ensures that each character's development and the plot's progression are coherent and logical. Similarly, GAAP ensures that financial statements are prepared consistently, making it easier for stakeholders to understand and compare them.

For instance, if a company changes its method of depreciation, GAAP requires that this change be disclosed and that the financial statements are adjusted to reflect this change. This is similar to how a script might adjust a subplot to ensure that it aligns with the main storyline, maintaining coherence and clarity.

Bollywood Dialogue: "Yeh kaisi baat kar rahe ho, tumhe bahut kuch sikhne ki zarurat hai" (*Kabhi Khushi Kabhie Gham*) – Just as this dialogue highlights the importance of learning and adapting, GAAP ensures that financial reporting adapts to maintain consistency and relevance.

1.3 IFRS (International Financial Reporting Standards)

Definition

International Financial Reporting Standards (IFRS) is a set of accounting standards developed and maintained by the International Accounting Standards Board (IASB). IFRS is used internationally and provides a uniform framework for financial reporting. The primary goal of IFRS is to ensure that financial statements are comparable across different countries, enhancing the transparency and reliability of financial information globally.

Key Aspects of IFRS

1. **Global Consistency**: IFRS aims to harmonize accounting practices across different countries. This global consistency helps multinational companies prepare their financial statements in a way that is understandable and comparable worldwide.
2. **Transparency**: IFRS enhances the transparency of financial reporting by requiring companies to provide detailed disclosures about their financial performance and position. This transparency helps investors and other stakeholders make more informed decisions.
3. **Accountability**: IFRS holds companies accountable for their financial reporting. By adhering to these standards, companies demonstrate their commitment to providing accurate and reliable financial information.
4. **Fair Presentation**: IFRS emphasizes the fair presentation of financial statements. This means that the financial statements should reflect the economic reality of the company, providing a true and fair view of its financial position and performance.

Example

Consider the Bollywood film *Lagaan*. The film's storyline, set in colonial India, needed to resonate with an international audience while staying true to its cultural roots. Just as *Lagaan* required a script and presentation that could appeal to viewers around the world, IFRS ensures that financial statements from different countries can be compared effectively.

For example, a multinational corporation with operations in both India and the United States would use IFRS to prepare its financial statements. This ensures that investors in both countries can understand and compare the company's financial performance and position, regardless of local accounting practices.

In *Lagaan*, the script and direction had to carefully balance local cultural elements with a narrative that could engage a global audience. Similarly, IFRS provides a common framework that helps bridge the gap between different national accounting practices, allowing for a uniform approach to financial reporting.

Bollywood Dialogue: "Bade bade deshon mein aisi choti choti baatein hoti rehti hain" (*Dilwale Dulhania Le Jayenge*) – Just as this dialogue reflects the complexity of relationships and the need to navigate intricate details, IFRS handles the complex details of international financial reporting, ensuring that financial statements from different countries align and can be compared effectively.

1.4 Conclusion

The script of a Bollywood film provides the essential framework for the story, guiding the plot, characters, and direction. Similarly, accounting principles like GAAP and

IFRS provide the framework for recording and reporting financial transactions. These principles ensure that financial statements are consistent, transparent, and comparable, allowing stakeholders to make informed decisions based on reliable information.

In this chapter, we have explored the fundamental principles of accounting through the lens of Bollywood. By drawing parallels between filmmaking and financial reporting, we have highlighted the importance of having a solid framework in place to ensure clarity and coherence. Just as a well-crafted script is crucial for a successful film, sound accounting principles are essential for accurate and reliable financial reporting.

As we continue our exploration of accounting concepts in the following chapters, we will delve deeper into how these principles come together to create a complete financial narrative. Just as every scene in a film contributes to the overall story, every accounting principle plays a crucial role in shaping the financial story of a business. Through Bollywood-inspired examples and dialogues, we aim to make these concepts more relatable and engaging, providing a comprehensive understanding of the art and science of accounting.

1.5 The Golden Rules of Accounting in Bollywood Style

Introduction: Accounting, much like the plots of Bollywood movies, follows a set of fundamental rules that ensure everything stays balanced and logical. These rules, known as the Golden Rules of Accounting, form the foundation for all financial transactions. Just as Bollywood directors adhere to certain formulas for creating hit films, accountants follow these rules to maintain the accuracy and integrity of financial records. Let's explore these rules through the lens of Bollywood, with examples that bring these concepts to life.

1. Golden Rule

A: Personal Accounts

Rule:*Debit the receiver, Credit the giver.*

Bollywood Style: Imagine a classic Bollywood scene where a kind-hearted hero (the giver) helps someone in need (the receiver). In accounting terms, whenever there's a transaction involving a person or an entity, the person receiving something is debited, and the person giving something is credited.

Example: In the film *"Munna Bhai M.B.B.S.,"* Munna (Sanjay Dutt) constantly helps others, offering his assistance to anyone in need. If Munna gives money to his friend Circuit (Arshad Warsi), Munna's account would be credited (since he's the giver), and Circuit's account would be debited (since he's the receiver).

This mirrors the accounting principle where if you pay someone, you credit your account (as you're the giver) and debit their account (as they're the receiver).

B: Real Accounts

Rule:*Debit what comes in, Credit what goes out.*

Bollywood Style: Think of a blockbuster Bollywood movie where the hero brings something valuable into his life or lets go of something significant. In accounting, this rule applies to assets or things of value. When something of value comes in, it is debited, and when it goes out, it is credited.

Example: In *"Dhoom 2,"* Hrithik Roshan's character, Aryan, pulls off a grand heist, bringing in valuable treasures. If Aryan acquires a priceless diamond, his asset account (the diamond) would be debited because something valuable has come in. If he then trades that diamond for something else, the diamond account would be credited (because it's going out), and the new asset would be debited.

In accounting, this is like buying equipment for your business: you debit the equipment account (because it's coming into your possession) and credit the cash account (because the money is going out).

C: Nominal Accounts

Rule:*Debit all expenses and losses, Credit all incomes and gains.*

Bollywood Style: Picture a Bollywood movie where the hero faces challenges (expenses and losses) but ultimately triumphs and reaps rewards (incomes and gains). This rule governs how we treat expenses, losses, incomes, and gains in accounting.

Example: In the movie *"Kabhi Khushi Kabhie Gham,"* the Raichand family experiences both joy and sorrow. When Yashvardhan Raichand (Amitabh Bachchan) spends money on his son's (Shah Rukh Khan) lavish wedding, those expenses are debited, reflecting the outflow of money. However, when the family business profits from a successful deal, that gain is credited, showing an inflow of wealth.

In accounting, paying rent for your office would result in debiting the rent expense account (a loss of money), while earning revenue from a sale would result in crediting the revenue account (a gain).

Conclusion:

Just like every Bollywood blockbuster follows a script to achieve its success, the Golden Rules of Accounting provide the script for managing financial transactions. By understanding these rules, you can ensure that every transaction is properly recorded, just as a Bollywood director ensures every scene contributes to the overall storyline.

So, whether you're watching a Bollywood film or balancing the books, remember: it's all about knowing the rules and playing your part to keep the story (or the finances) moving smoothly!

1.6 Summary

1. **Accounting Principles as a Script**: Like a movie script, accounting principles ensure consistency, accuracy, and transparency in financial reporting.
2. **GAAP**: U.S.-based guidelines that provide structure, ensuring reliability and comparability in financial statements.
3. **IFRS**: Global standards for consistent and transparent financial reporting across different countries.
4. **Golden Rules of Accounting**: Comparable to Bollywood formulas, these rules guide financial transactions, such as debiting the receiver and crediting the giver.
5. **Overall Importance**: These principles and rules are essential for maintaining clarity and reliability in financial statements, just as a solid script is crucial for a successful film.

CHAPTER TWO

The Director - The Accountant

2.1 Introduction

"Don ka intezaar toh gyarah mulkon ki police kar rahi hai, lekin Don ko pakadna mushkil hi nahi, namumkin hai." – Don

An accountant is like Don – the one who controls the entire financial story. "Balance sheet ka hisaab karna mushkil hi nahi, namumkin hai" without a good accountant. Just as the director ensures that every scene aligns with the movie's script, the accountant ensures that every financial transaction is accurately recorded and reported. "Kyunki accountant ka kaam hai sab kuch pakka karna!"

In the world of Bollywood, the director is the linchpin of a film's success. Responsible for translating the script into a captivating visual experience, the director oversees every aspect of filmmaking, ensuring that each scene aligns with the overarching vision of the story. Much like the director's role in filmmaking, an accountant is pivotal in the realm of financial reporting. The accountant's job is to ensure that each financial transaction is recorded accurately, decisions about financial reporting are made judiciously, and ethical standards are upheld to maintain transparency and fairness. This chapter delves into the multifaceted role of an accountant, drawing parallels with the director's role in filmmaking to provide a comprehensive understanding of accounting responsibilities, decision-making, and ethics.

2.2 Responsibilities of an Accountant

Definition

The core responsibilities of an accountant encompass recording, classifying, and summarizing financial transactions. This foundational work is critical for producing accurate financial statements and reports, which are essential for decision-making by stakeholders, including management, investors, and regulators.

Recording Transactions

The first responsibility of an accountant is to record every financial transaction in the company's books. This involves documenting each transaction accurately and timely, ensuring that the financial records are complete and up-to-date. Recording transactions includes entries such as sales, purchases, expenses, and payments.

Classifying Transactions

After transactions are recorded, they need to be classified into appropriate categories. Classification involves grouping similar transactions into accounts, such as assets, liabilities, equity, revenue, and expenses. This process helps in organizing the financial information systematically, making it easier to prepare financial statements.

Summarizing Transactions

Summarizing involves aggregating the classified data to prepare financial statements. This includes creating a balance sheet, income statement, and cash flow statement. Summarization ensures that the financial information is presented clearly and concisely, providing a snapshot of the company's financial position and performance.

Example

Consider the film *3 Idiots*, where the director, Rajkumar Hirani, plays a crucial role in ensuring that each scene contributes to the film's overall message of pursuing one's passion. Similarly, an accountant's role is to ensure that each financial transaction is accurately recorded, classified, and summarized. Just as Hirani ensures that every scene aligns with the film's theme of education and personal growth, the accountant ensures that each transaction aligns with the company's financial reporting requirements.

For instance, if a company purchases new equipment, the accountant will record this transaction in the appropriate asset account, classify it under capital expenditures, and summarize it in the financial statements. This process ensures that the financial reports reflect the true state of the company's assets and investments.

Bollywood Dialogue: "All is well" (*3 Idiots*) – Just as this dialogue conveys reassurance and trust in a complex situation, accurate and thorough recording, classification, and summarization of financial transactions ensure the reliability of financial statements.

2.3 Decision-Making

Definition

Decision-making in accounting involves determining how to classify and report financial transactions. This includes selecting appropriate accounting methods, estimates, and judgments to present a true and fair view of the company's financial position and performance.

Classification Decisions

Accountants must decide how to classify transactions into various accounts. For example, an expense might be classified as either an operating expense or a capital expenditure, depending on its nature and impact on the financial statements.

Reporting Decisions

Reporting decisions involve choosing how to present financial information. This includes selecting accounting methods for revenue recognition, inventory valuation, and depreciation. Accountants must ensure that these choices comply with accounting standards and provide a true representation of the company's financial status.

Example

In *Chakde! India*, the director, Shimit Amin, makes critical decisions about how to shoot and edit each scene to effectively convey the film's message of teamwork and perseverance. Similarly, an accountant makes decisions about how to report financial transactions to present a clear and accurate picture of the company's financial health.

For instance, if a company needs to decide between different methods of inventory valuation (such as FIFO or LIFO), the accountant must choose the method that best reflects the company's financial performance and position. This decision impacts the cost of goods sold, net income, and inventory valuation on the balance sheet.

Bollywood Dialogue: "Agar tumhare paas time nahi hai toh mujhe kyun pareshan kar rahe ho?" (*Chakde! India*) – Just as this dialogue emphasizes making the right choices in critical moments, accountants must make informed decisions to ensure accurate financial reporting.

2.4 Ethics

Definition

Ethics in accounting involves adhering to professional standards and principles to ensure fairness, objectivity, and integrity in financial reporting. Accountants must avoid conflicts of interest, manipulation, and misrepresentation to maintain the trust and credibility of financial information.

Professional Integrity

Accountants must demonstrate honesty and integrity in their work. This involves providing accurate and truthful information, even when it might not be favorable to the company. Professional integrity ensures that financial statements are reliable and trustworthy.

Avoiding Manipulation

Accountants must avoid any form of financial manipulation or "creative accounting" that might distort the true financial position of the company. This includes avoiding practices such as inflating revenues or concealing expenses to present a more favorable financial picture.

Adherence to Standards

Accountants must adhere to ethical standards set by professional bodies, such as the American Institute of Certified Public Accountants (AICPA) or the International Federation of Accountants (IFAC). These standards provide guidelines for ethical behaviour and professional conduct in accounting.

Example

In the iconic Bollywood film *Sholay*, the character Thakur Baldev Singh adheres to moral values and justice, which are central to his role in the story. Similarly, accountants must uphold ethical standards to ensure that financial reporting is transparent and fair. Just as Thakur's adherence to values drives the narrative, adherence to ethics drives the credibility of financial reporting.

For instance, if an accountant is aware of potential fraudulent activities within the company, they must report these issues rather than ignoring or concealing them. This ensures that stakeholders are informed of any significant issues that might affect the company's financial health.

Bollywood Dialogue: "Kitne aadmi the?" (*Sholay*) – This iconic question checks for authenticity and truthfulness in a tense situation. Similarly, accounting ethics ensure that financial reporting remains transparent and free from manipulation, upholding the integrity of financial information.

2.5 Conclusion

Just as the director is crucial for executing the vision of a film, ensuring that each scene aligns with the script, the accountant plays a pivotal role in financial reporting. By recording, classifying, and summarizing financial transactions, making informed decisions, and adhering to ethical standards, accountants ensure that financial statements are accurate, reliable, and fair.

In this chapter, we have explored the multifaceted role of the accountant through the lens of Bollywood filmmaking. By drawing parallels between the director's role and the accountant's responsibilities, decision-making, and ethics, we have provided a comprehensive understanding of the critical functions that underpin effective financial reporting.

As we continue our exploration of accounting concepts in the subsequent chapters, we will delve deeper into how these principles and practices come together to create a complete financial narrative. Just as every decision made by a director impacts the overall film, every decision made by an accountant impacts the accuracy and integrity of financial reporting. Through Bollywood-inspired examples and dialogues, we aim to make these concepts more relatable and engaging, providing a deeper appreciation for the art and science of accounting.

1. **Summary**

1. Accountant as Director: An accountant, like a film director, ensures every financial transaction is accurately recorded and reported.

2. Responsibilities: Accountants record, classify, and summarize financial transactions to produce accurate financial statements.

3. Decision-Making: Accountants make crucial decisions about how to classify and report transactions, ensuring compliance with standards.

4. Ethics: Upholding ethical standards, accountants avoid manipulation and ensure transparency in financial reporting.

5. Conclusion: Accountants play a pivotal role in financial reporting, much like a director ensures a film's success by aligning every scene with the script.

CHAPTER THREE

The Cast - Assets, Liabilities, and Equity

3.1 Introduction

"Mere paas maa hai." – Deewar

In the accounting world, if assets say "Mere paas maa hai", liabilities and equity respond with "Mere paas balance sheet ka pura record hai!"

- Assets are like the hero, carrying the story forward. Cash, property, inventory – "sab kuch hai mere paas!"
- Liabilities: "Main villain hoon, lekin bina mere kahani adhoori hai." Debts and obligations are necessary, just like a villain to make the story interesting.
- Equity: "Jo mere saath hai, wahi asli hero hai." Equity represents the owners' claim on the company, the real strength behind the business.

In Bollywood, the cast is integral to a film's success, each actor bringing unique qualities and depth to their role. Similarly, in accounting, the financial "cast" comprises Assets, Liabilities, and Equity. These elements form the backbone of the financial statements, shaping the narrative of a company's economic health. This chapter delves into each component in detail, exploring their definitions, characteristics, and roles in the financial story of a business, illustrated with Bollywood-themed examples.

3.2 Assets

Definition

Assets are resources owned by a company that are expected to provide future economic benefits. They are crucial for generating revenue and supporting operations. Assets can be tangible, such as cash or equipment, or intangible, such as patents or trademarks.

Examples

1. **Cash**

Definition: Cash includes funds available for immediate use, such as currency, bank deposits, and cheques. It is the most liquid asset and is vital for day-to-day operations.

Bollywood Example: In *Jab Tak Hai Jaan*, the protagonist's wealth and resources play a significant role in the storyline. Imagine the cash reserves as the treasure in the film – a crucial resource that provides financial stability and flexibility. Just as cash enables characters to pursue their goals and support their loved ones, cash in a business enables operations, investments, and growth.

Accounting Context: On the balance sheet, cash is listed under current assets, reflecting its liquidity and availability for short-term needs. Effective cash management is essential for ensuring that the company can meet its immediate obligations and invest in opportunities.

1. Inventory

Definition: Inventory consists of goods and materials a company holds for the purpose of resale or production. It includes finished goods, raw materials, and work-in-progress.

Bollywood Example: In *Dhoom 2*, the valuable items and artifacts featured in the heist are akin to a company's inventory. Just as these items are central to the plot and have significant value, inventory in a business represents valuable resources that will be sold to generate revenue.

Accounting Context: Inventory is categorized as a current asset on the balance sheet. It is crucial for a business to manage inventory levels effectively to balance supply and demand, avoid stockouts, and reduce holding costs.

3. Property, Plant, and Equipment (PP&E)

Definition: PP&E includes long-term assets like land, buildings, machinery, and equipment used in production and operations. These assets have a useful life extending beyond one year.

Bollywood Example: In *Chakde! India*, the hockey field and equipment are essential to the team's success. Similarly, PP&E in a business supports long-term operations and productivity. Just as the hockey field is a vital asset for the team, PP&E is crucial for a company's operational capacity.

Accounting Context: PP&E is recorded at historical cost and depreciated over its useful life. This process allocates the cost of the asset over its life, reflecting its usage and wear-and-tear.

4. Intangible Assets

Definition: Intangible assets are non-physical assets that provide value to the company. They include patents, trademarks, copyrights, and goodwill.

Bollywood Example: In *Guru*, the protagonist's business acumen and innovative ideas are intangible assets that drive the success of his enterprise. Similarly, intangible assets in a business, such as intellectual property and brand value, play a significant role in its competitive advantage and market position.

Accounting Context: Intangible assets are recorded at cost and amortized over their useful life. Unlike tangible assets, intangible assets do not have physical substance but can significantly impact a company's value and profitability.

3.3 Liabilities

Definition

Liabilities are obligations or debts that a company owes to external parties. They represent claims against the company's assets and are essential for understanding a company's financial obligations and leverage.

Examples

1. Accounts Payable

Definition: Accounts payable represents amounts a company owes to suppliers for goods and services received but not yet paid for. It is a short-term liability.

Bollywood Example: In *Deewar*, the debts and obligations faced by the characters reflect the financial strain and responsibility they carry. Similarly, accounts payable represents the company's short-term obligations to its suppliers, crucial for managing cash flow and maintaining supplier relationships.

Accounting Context: Accounts payable is listed under current liabilities on the balance sheet. Managing accounts payable effectively ensures that the company meets its short-term obligations while optimizing cash flow.

2. Loans Payable

Definition: Loans payable are amounts borrowed by the company that need to be repaid over time. These can be short-term or long-term liabilities, depending on the repayment period.

Bollywood Example: In *Chakde! India*, the significant loans and financial commitments taken on by the characters are crucial to the plot. They represent substantial financial obligations that impact the team's ability to succeed. Similarly, loans payable are major financial commitments that affect a company's financial stability and long-term planning.

Accounting Context: Loans payable are classified as either short-term or long-term liabilities based on the repayment schedule. Effective management of loans payable involves monitoring interest payments, repayment schedules, and the impact on overall financial health.

3. Accrued Expenses

Definition: Accrued expenses are costs that have been incurred but not yet paid. They are recorded as liabilities until the payment is made.

Bollywood Example: In *Lagaan*, the preparation for the cricket match involves various costs that are incurred before they are paid. Similarly, accrued expenses represent costs that a company has incurred but has not yet settled, impacting financial reporting and budgeting.

Accounting Context: Accrued expenses are listed under current liabilities. Properly accounting for accrued expenses ensures that financial statements reflect the true expenses incurred during a period, providing an accurate view of financial performance.

3.4 Equity

Definition

Equity represents the owners' residual interest in the company after all liabilities have been settled. It reflects the ownership value and residual claim on the company's assets and profits.

Examples

1. **Common Stock**

Definition: Common stock represents ownership shares issued to investors. It reflects the capital invested by shareholders in exchange for equity ownership in the company.

Bollywood Example: In *Guru*, the protagonist's stake in his business represents his ownership and investment. Similarly, common stock reflects shareholders' ownership in a company and their claim on the company's profits and assets.

Accounting Context: Common stock is recorded in the equity section of the balance sheet. It represents the capital raised from shareholders and is essential for understanding the ownership structure and financial backing of the company.

2. Retained Earnings

Definition: Retained earnings are the accumulated profits of a company that have been reinvested in the business rather than distributed as dividends. It reflects the company's ability to generate and retain profits over time.

Bollywood Example: In *Lagaan*, the reinvestment of resources and efforts towards the cricket match symbolizes the retention of profits for future growth. Similarly, retained earnings represent the portion of profits reinvested in the business to support expansion, research, and development.

Accounting Context: Retained earnings are recorded in the equity section of the balance sheet. They provide insights into the company's profitability and its approach to profit distribution and reinvestment.

3. Additional Paid-in Capital

Definition: Additional paid-in capital represents the amount paid by shareholders over and above the par value of common stock. It reflects extra capital contributed by investors beyond the nominal value of shares.

Bollywood Example: In *Chakde! India*, the additional support and investments from various sources beyond the immediate needs of the team symbolize additional paid-in capital. Similarly, this component of equity reflects extra capital raised from shareholders beyond the basic stock issuance.

Accounting Context: Additional paid-in capital is recorded in the equity section of the balance sheet. It represents additional funds contributed by shareholders and reflects the company's ability to attract investment and support its growth.

Bollywood Dialogue: "Mere paas maa hai" (*Deewar*) – This iconic dialogue highlights the value and support provided by a mother, much like how assets support business operations. In the same vein, equity represents the essential support and value that shareholders and retained earnings provide to the company.

3.5 Conclusion

Just as the cast in Bollywood brings a film to life, Assets, Liabilities, and Equity are essential components that shape a company's financial narrative. Each element plays a crucial role in the financial story, providing insights into the company's resources, obligations, and ownership value. By understanding these components, we gain a clearer picture of the company's financial health and performance.

In this chapter, we have explored the fundamental elements of the financial cast, illustrated with Bollywood-themed examples to make these concepts relatable and engaging. As we continue to explore accounting concepts in the subsequent chapters, we will further examine how these elements interact and contribute to the overall financial story of a business. Just as each actor's role contributes to the success of a film, each component of the financial cast plays a critical role in presenting an accurate and comprehensive financial picture.

3.6 Summary

1. **Introduction**: Assets, Liabilities, and Equity are like the cast in a movie, each playing a vital role in a company's financial story.
2. **Assets**: Represent resources owned by a company, like cash, inventory, and equipment, driving business operations.
3. **Liabilities**: Reflect obligations or debts the company owes, essential for understanding financial obligations and leverage.
4. **Equity**: Represents the owners' claim on the company after liabilities, indicating ownership value and financial strength.
5. **Conclusion**: These elements form the backbone of financial statements, shaping the narrative of a company's economic health, similar to how actors shape a film's success.

CHAPTER FOUR

The Plot – The Accounting Equation

4.1 Introduction

"Rishtey mein toh hum tumhare baap lagte hain, naam hai Shehenshah." – Shehenshah

The accounting equation is the ultimate Shehenshah: "Assets = Liabilities + Equity." It's the relationship that governs everything in accounting. No matter what happens, this equation must always balance, because "balance sheet ka hisaab hamesha barabar hona chahiye!"

In filmmaking, the plot is the central thread that ties together all elements of the story—characters, settings, and events—into a coherent and engaging narrative. It ensures that every scene, dialogue, and subplot contributes to the overall story arc. Similarly, in financial accounting, the Accounting Equation serves as the fundamental framework that maintains balance and coherence in financial reporting. This equation is essential for understanding how a company's resources are financed and how its financial statements are interrelated. This chapter delves into the Accounting Equation, its significance, and its role in ensuring balanced financial statements, illustrated with Bollywood-themed examples to bring the concept to life.

4.2 The Accounting Equation

Definition

The Accounting Equation is a fundamental principle in accounting that states:

Assets=Liabilities+Equity

This equation serves as the foundation for the double-entry bookkeeping system, ensuring that a company's financial statements remain balanced. It reflects the relationship between what a company owns (its assets), what it owes (its liabilities), and the owners' residual interest in the company (equity). The equation must always be in balance, meaning that the total value of assets must equal the sum of liabilities and equity.

Significance of the Accounting Equation

1. **Ensuring Balance**

The Accounting Equation ensures that every financial transaction is recorded in such a way that the company's balance sheet remains balanced. This balance is crucial for accurate financial reporting and analysis. For example, if a company acquires a new asset, the increase in assets must be offset by an equal increase in liabilities, equity, or both, to maintain equilibrium.

1. **Reflecting Financial Health**

By maintaining this balance, the Accounting Equation provides a clear picture of a company's financial health.

It allows stakeholders to understand how the company's assets are financed—whether through debt, equity, or a combination of both. This insight is essential for assessing the company's financial stability, liquidity, and capital structure.

3. Facilitating Accurate Reporting

The equation helps in accurate financial reporting by ensuring that all transactions are properly recorded and that the financial statements are complete and correct. It serves as a check-and-balance mechanism that helps prevent errors and discrepancies in financial reporting.

Bollywood Example: Buying Equipment

Imagine a company decides to purchase a new piece of equipment worth $10,000. The company pays $4,000 in cash and takes out a $6,000 loan to cover the remaining amount. In this scenario, the Accounting Equation is used to ensure that the transaction is accurately reflected in the financial statements.

- **Assets**: The company's assets increase by $10,000 due to the acquisition of the new equipment.
- **Liabilities**: The company's liabilities increase by $6,000 due to the new loan.
- **Equity**: The cash payment of $4,000 reduces the company's cash balance, but the equity remains unchanged because the equipment is financed partly by a loan and partly by cash.

Accounting Equation Breakdown:

- **Before the Transaction:**

- ◦ Assets = Liabilities + Equity
- ◦ Suppose the company's initial balance is:

  - ▪ Assets = $50,000 (Including Cash)
  - ▪ Liabilities = $20,000
  - ▪ Equity = $30,000

- **After the Transaction:**

  - ◦ The new equipment is added to assets: $50,000 + $10,000 = $60,000
  - ◦ The loan increases liabilities: $20,000 + $6,000 = $26,000
  - ◦ Cash is decreased by $4,000 from assets: $60,000 - $4,000 = $56,000
  - ◦ Therefore:

    - ▪ New Assets = $56,000
    - ▪ New Liabilities = $26,000
    - ▪ New Equity = $30,000

  - ◦ The equation remains balanced:

    - ▪ $56,000 (Assets) = $26,000 (Liabilities) + $30,000 (Equity)

Just as the plot in *Zindagi Na Milegi Dobara* weaves together diverse storylines into a cohesive narrative, the Accounting Equation integrates various financial elements into a balanced and comprehensive financial picture.

Bollywood Dialogue: "Jo jeeta wahi sikandar" (*Jo Jeeta Wohi Sikandar*)

This iconic dialogue translates to "The one who wins is the conqueror," reflecting the importance of balance and strategy in achieving success. Similarly, the Accounting Equation ensures balance in financial reporting, which is crucial for accurate and reliable financial statements. Just as a well-balanced strategy leads to victory in a race, a balanced Accounting Equation ensures that financial statements accurately reflect a company's financial position and performance.

4.3 Practical Application of the Accounting Equation

Recording Transactions

Every financial transaction affects the Accounting Equation and must be recorded in such a way that the equation remains balanced. Here's how different types of transactions impact the equation:

1. Asset Purchase

When a company buys an asset, it can either use cash, take out a loan, or issue equity. Each method affects the Accounting Equation differently but maintains balance:

- **Cash Purchase**: Reduces cash (an asset) but increases another asset (e.g., inventory or equipment).

    - Example: Buying inventory worth $5,000 using cash:

- Assets: Cash decreases by $5,000, inventory increases by $5,000.
- Liabilities and Equity remain unchanged.

- **Loan Financing**: Increases assets and liabilities.

  - Example: Purchasing equipment worth $10,000 with a $7,000 loan:

    - Assets: Equipment increases by $10,000, cash decreases by $3,000.
    - Liabilities: Loan payable increases by $7,000.
    - Equity remains unchanged.

- **Equity Financing**: Increases assets and equity.

  - Example: Issuing common stock for $8,000:

    - Assets: Cash increases by $8,000.
    - Equity: Common stock increases by $8,000.

2. Revenue Recognition

When a company earns revenue, it either receives cash or generates accounts receivable:

- **Cash Revenue**: Increases cash and equity.

  - Example: Earning $4,000 in cash:

    - Assets: Cash increases by $4,000.
    - Equity: Retained earnings increase by $4,000.

- ○ **Credit Revenue**: Increases accounts receivable and equity.

  - Example: Earning $2,000 on credit:

    - Assets: Accounts receivable increases by $2,000.
    - Equity: Retained earnings increase by $2,000.

3. **Expense Recognition**

When a company incurs expenses, it decreases assets or increases liabilities, impacting equity:

- ○ **Cash Expenses**: Reduces cash and equity.

  - Example: Paying $1,500 for utilities:

    - Assets: Cash decreases by $1,500.
    - Equity: Retained earnings decrease by $1,500.

- ○ **Accrued Expenses**: Increases liabilities and decreases equity.

  - Example: Incurred $1,200 in salaries payable:

    - Liabilities: Salaries payable increases by $1,200.
    - Equity: Retained earnings decrease by $1,200.

4.4 Impact on Financial Statements

The Accounting Equation impacts the preparation of key financial statements:

1. Balance Sheet

The balance sheet, also known as the statement of financial position, provides a snapshot of a company's assets, liabilities, and equity at a specific point in time. The Accounting Equation forms the basis of this statement, ensuring that total assets equal the sum of liabilities and equity.

2. Income Statement

The income statement, or profit and loss statement, shows the company's revenues and expenses over a period, ultimately affecting equity. The net income or loss from the income statement is transferred to retained earnings in the equity section of the balance sheet.

3. Cash Flow Statement

The cash flow statement outlines the cash inflows and outflows from operating, investing, and financing activities. It provides insights into how cash is generated and used, impacting the cash component of assets and indirectly affecting the balance between assets, liabilities, and equity.

A. Cahs flow from Operating Activities

The concept of cash flow from operating activities is quite similar to that of Operating Income. The goal is to measure the cash flow that is the result of activities directly related to normal business operations. (i.e. things that will likely be repeated year after year).

Common items that are categorised as cash flow from operating activities include:

1. Receipts from the sale of goods and services
2. Payments made to suppliers
3. Payment made to employees
4. Payment made as Tax payments

B. Cash flow from Investing Activities

Cash flow from Investing activities includes cash spent on or received from investment in financial securities (stock, bonds etc.) as well as cash spend on or received from capital assets (assets expected to last longer than one year)

Common items that are categorised as cash flow from Investing activities include:

1. Purchase or sale of property, plant or equipment
2. Purchase or sale of stock
3. Interest or Dividend received from investments

C. Cash flow from Financing Activities

Cahs flow from Financing activities includes cash inflow and outflow relating to transaction with company's owners and creditors.

Common items that are categorised as cash flow from Investing activities include:

1. Dividend paid to shareholders

2. Cash flow related to taking out or paying back a loan
3. Cash received from investor when new shares of stock are issued

4.5 Conclusion

The Accounting Equation is the backbone of financial accounting, ensuring that every transaction is recorded in a manner that maintains balance and coherence in financial reporting. Just as the plot in Bollywood connects all elements of the story into a unified narrative, the Accounting Equation integrates various financial transactions into a balanced and accurate financial picture.

By understanding and applying the Accounting Equation, businesses can ensure that their financial statements are accurate, complete, and reflective of their true financial position. This balance is crucial for making informed business decisions, securing financing, and communicating financial performance to stakeholders. As we continue to explore accounting concepts, we will see how the Accounting Equation interacts with other elements of financial reporting, further illustrating the importance of maintaining balance in the financial narrative.

4.6 Summary

1. **Introduction**: The Accounting Equation, "Assets = Liabilities + Equity," is the core principle in accounting, ensuring balance in financial reporting.
2. **Significance:**

- Ensures that the balance sheet remains balanced after every transaction.
- Reflects the company's financial health by showing how assets are financed.
- Facilitates accurate and reliable financial reporting.

3. **Practical Application**: Different transactions (asset purchases, revenue, and expenses) impact the equation but maintain balance.
4. **Impact**: The equation forms the basis for key financial statements: balance sheet, income statement, and cash flow statement.
5. **Conclusion**: The Accounting Equation is essential for accurate financial reporting and maintaining balance in the financial narrative.

CHAPTER FIVE

Scenes – Financial Transactions

5.1 Introduction

"Mogambo khush hua!" – Mr. India

Every financial transaction is a key scene in the company's story. When sales happen, "Mogambo khush hota hai!" because it means more revenue. Whether it's buying new equipment or paying salaries, each transaction must be recorded to keep the story moving forward.

In the world of filmmaking, every scene plays a pivotal role in advancing the plot, shaping characters, and delivering the overall message of the film. Each scene is carefully crafted to contribute to the narrative, creating a cohesive and engaging story. Similarly, in financial accounting, every financial transaction is a critical event that affects the company's financial statements and overall financial position. This chapter explores the importance of financial transactions, how they are recorded, and their impact on a company's financial narrative, drawing parallels with Bollywood films to illustrate these concepts.

5.2 Financial Transactions

Definition

Financial transactions are events that have a financial impact on a company's financial statements. These transactions affect various elements of the financial statements, such as assets, liabilities, equity, revenues, and expenses. Recording these transactions accurately is essential for maintaining the integrity of financial reporting and providing a true and fair view of the company's financial position.

Examples

1. **Sale of Goods**

When a company sells goods, it generates revenue, which is recognized in the financial statements. The sale impacts both the income statement and the balance sheet:

- **Revenue Recognition**: Revenue is recorded when it is earned, regardless of when the cash is received. This aligns with the accrual basis of accounting.
- **Accounts Receivable or Cash**: Depending on whether the sale is made on credit or for cash, either accounts receivable or cash is updated.

Bollywood Parallel: *Kabir Singh*

In *Kabir Singh*, pivotal scenes drive the plot forward, such as when Kabir's actions significantly alter his life's direction. Similarly, a sale of goods is a crucial financial transaction that shifts the company's financial trajectory by increasing revenue and affecting cash flow or accounts receivable.

Example Calculation:

- ○ Sale of goods worth $5,000 on credit:

    - **Debit Accounts Receivable**: $5,000
    - **Credit Revenue**: $5,000

This transaction shows an increase in accounts receivable and revenue, reflecting the company's growing sales and potential future cash inflows.

1. **Purchase of Supplies**

When a company purchases supplies or inventory, it affects the expenses and inventory accounts. This transaction is recorded as follows:

- ○ **Expense Recording**: If the supplies are consumed immediately, they are recorded as an expense.
- ○ **Inventory Update**: If the supplies are held for future use, they are recorded as inventory.

Bollywood Parallel: *Dil Chahta Hai*
In *Dil Chahta Hai*, character development scenes reveal the personal growth and changes in the characters' lives. Similarly, the purchase of supplies or inventory impacts the financial statements by updating expenses or inventory and shaping the company's cost structure.
Example Calculation:

- ○ Purchase of supplies worth $2,000:

- **Debit Inventory**: $2,000 (if supplies are held for future use)
- **Credit Accounts Payable**: $2,000

If the supplies are consumed immediately:

- **Debit Expense**: $2,000
- **Credit Accounts Payable**: $2,000

This transaction reflects the company's investment in resources and its obligations to pay suppliers.

5.3 Impact on Financial Statements

1. **Income Statement**

Financial transactions affect the income statement by altering revenues and expenses. Sales transactions increase revenues, while purchases and other expenses reduce profits. Accurate recording of these transactions is vital for reflecting the company's performance over a period.

2. **Balance Sheet**

Transactions also impact the balance sheet by altering assets, liabilities, and equity. For instance, sales increase accounts receivable or cash (assets), while purchases increase inventory (assets) or accounts payable (liabilities). Ensuring that these transactions are correctly recorded maintains the balance between assets, liabilities, and equity.

3. Cash Flow Statement

The cash flow statement is affected by transactions involving cash inflows and outflows. Sales that result in cash receipts increase cash flow from operating activities, while purchases of supplies or inventory affect cash outflows. Accurate tracking of these transactions is essential for managing cash flow and liquidity.

5.4 Recording Transactions

Definition

Recording transactions involves documenting each financial event using the double-entry accounting system. This method ensures that every transaction affects at least two accounts, maintaining the balance of the Accounting Equation (Assets = Liabilities + Equity). The double-entry system relies on debits and credits to record transactions accurately.

Examples

1. Recording a Sale

When a sale occurs, the following entries are made:

- **Debit Accounts Receivable or Cash**: Increases assets.
- **Credit Revenue**: Increases equity through retained earnings.

Example Calculation:

- Sale of $5,000 on credit:

- **Debit Accounts Receivable**: $5,000
- **Credit Revenue**: $5,000

This entry reflects an increase in assets (accounts receivable) and revenue, impacting both the balance sheet and the income statement.

2. **Recording a Purchase**

When purchasing supplies or inventory:

- **Debit Inventory**: Increases assets.
- **Credit Accounts Payable**: Increases liabilities.

Example Calculation:

- Purchase of $2,000 in supplies:

    - **Debit Inventory**: $2,000 (if supplies are held)
    - **Credit Accounts Payable**: $2,000

If the supplies are used immediately:

- **Debit Expense**: $2,000
- **Credit Accounts Payable**: $2,000

These entries reflect the acquisition of resources and the obligation to pay suppliers, impacting the balance sheet and expense reporting.

Bollywood Dialogue: "Aaj mere paas gaadi hai, bungalow hai, bank balance hai, kya hai tumhare paas?" (*Deewar*)

This famous dialogue translates to "Today, I have a car, a bungalow, a bank balance—what do you have?" It emphasizes the accumulation of assets and financial achievements. Similarly, every financial transaction adds to the company's financial narrative, reflecting changes in assets, liabilities, and equity. Just as each scene in a movie contributes to the overall story, each transaction adds to the company's financial story, shaping its economic reality and performance.

5.5 Conclusion

Financial transactions are the building blocks of a company's financial narrative, much like scenes in a Bollywood film contribute to the overall plot. Each transaction affects various aspects of the financial statements, including assets, liabilities, equity, revenues, and expenses. Accurate recording of these transactions using the double-entry accounting system ensures that financial statements are balanced and reflective of the company's true financial position.

By understanding the impact of financial transactions and their proper recording, businesses can maintain accurate and reliable financial records, which are essential for decision-making, financial analysis, and reporting. Just as each scene in a film plays a crucial role in advancing the plot and developing characters, each financial transaction plays a vital role in shaping the company's financial story and ensuring a coherent and balanced financial report.

5.6 Summary

1. **Introduction**: Financial transactions are key events that impact a company's financial story, similar to pivotal scenes in a film.
2. **Financial Transactions**:

   - Affect assets, liabilities, equity, revenue, and expenses.
   - Examples include the sale of goods and the purchase of supplies, which influence financial statements.

3. **Impact**:

   - **Income Statement**: Alters revenues and expenses.
   - **Balance Sheet**: Changes assets, liabilities, and equity.
   - **Cash Flow Statement**: Reflects cash inflows and outflows.

4. **Recording**: Uses double-entry accounting to ensure every transaction balances the Accounting Equation.
5. **Conclusion**: Accurate transaction recording is crucial for maintaining balanced and reliable financial statements, shaping the company's financial narrative.

CHAPTER SIX

The Film Reel - The Ledger

6.1 Introduction

"Picture abhi baaki hai, mere dost!" – Om Shanti Om

The ledger is where all the action happens. It's the reel that holds the entire movie together. Every financial transaction is recorded here, "kyunki picture abhi baaki hai, aur yeh ledger puri kahani sunayega." It ensures that everything is accounted for and that the story remains consistent.

In filmmaking, the film reel is crucial as it holds all the recorded scenes, capturing every moment and detail of the story. This reel ensures that every scene, shot, and dialogue contributes to the final narrative, providing a complete picture of the film's storyline. Similarly, in accounting, the ledger functions as the comprehensive record of all financial transactions, capturing every detail of a company's financial activities. This chapter delves into the role of the ledger in accounting, comparing its importance to the film reel in filmmaking. By examining the different types of ledgers and their functions, we can understand how they contribute to accurate and reliable financial reporting.

6.2 The Ledger

Definition

The ledger is a crucial component of the accounting system, serving as the central repository where all financial transactions are recorded and organized. It provides a detailed and systematic record of all financial activities, ensuring that each transaction is captured and classified appropriately. The ledger helps in maintaining the integrity of the financial reporting process by consolidating all transactions into a coherent and accessible format.

Examples

1. General Ledger

The general ledger is the primary ledger that includes all the accounts needed to prepare financial statements. It encompasses various categories of accounts, such as assets, liabilities, equity, revenues, and expenses. Each account within the general ledger contains a record of all transactions related to that particular category.

- **Asset Accounts**: Include cash, accounts receivable, inventory, and fixed assets.
- **Liability Accounts**: Include accounts payable, loans payable, and accrued expenses.
- **Equity Accounts**: Include common stock, retained earnings, and additional paid-in capital.
- **Revenue Accounts**: Include sales revenue, interest income, and other revenue streams.

- ○ **Expense Accounts**: Include salaries expense, rent expense, and utility expense.

Bollywood Parallel: *Dilwale Dulhania Le Jayenge*

Just as the general ledger captures all the key elements of the film's story, including the lead characters, their relationships, and pivotal events, the general ledger consolidates all account transactions, providing a complete financial picture of the company.

Example Calculation:

- ○ **Asset Account (Cash):**

    - ▪ **Debit**: $10,000 (Increase in cash from a sale)
    - ▪ **Credit**: $5,000 (Decrease in cash from a purchase)

- ○ **Liability Account (Accounts Payable):**

    - ▪ **Debit**: $2,000 (Payment to a supplier)
    - ▪ **Credit**: $4,000 (New purchase on credit)

These entries illustrate how transactions are recorded in various accounts, contributing to the overall financial statements.

1. **Subsidiary Ledgers**

Subsidiary ledgers provide detailed records for specific areas of the general ledger, offering more granular information on particular accounts. They support the general ledger by breaking down data into more manageable segments.

- ○ **Accounts Receivable Ledger**: Contains detailed records of amounts owed by customers. Each entry reflects individual customer transactions and outstanding balances.
- ○ **Accounts Payable Ledger**: Contains detailed records of amounts owed to suppliers. Each entry tracks payments and outstanding amounts to various vendors.

Bollywood Parallel: *Kabhi Khushi Kabhie Gham*

In *Kabhi Khushi Kabhie Gham*, the story is enriched by detailed subplots and character interactions that contribute to the overall narrative. Similarly, subsidiary ledgers provide detailed insights into specific areas of the company's financial activities, adding depth and clarity to the general ledger.

Example Calculation:

- ○ **Accounts Receivable Ledger:**

  - **Customer A:**

    - **Debit:** $1,000 (Sale on credit)
    - **Credit:** $500 (Payment received)

  - **Customer B:**

    - **Debit:** $2,000 (Sale on credit)
    - **Credit:** $1,000 (Payment received)

- ○ **Accounts Payable Ledger:**

  - **Supplier X:**

- **Debit:** $1,500 (Payment made)
- **Credit:** $2,000 (Purchase on credit)

- **Supplier Y:**

  - **Debit:** $800 (Payment made)
  - **Credit:** $1,200 (Purchase on credit)

These entries illustrate how subsidiary ledgers track detailed transactions, supporting the general ledger's overall accuracy.

6.3 Role in Financial Reporting

1. Accuracy and Reconciliation

The ledger plays a vital role in ensuring the accuracy and completeness of financial reporting. By recording every transaction in the appropriate accounts, the ledger helps reconcile financial data, ensuring that the total debits equal total credits. This reconciliation process is essential for detecting and correcting errors, maintaining the integrity of the financial statements.

Bollywood Parallel: *Chakde! India*

In *Chakde! India*, every match and training session is meticulously planned and executed to ensure the team's success. Similarly, the ledger ensures that every financial transaction is accurately recorded and reconciled, contributing to the overall accuracy of the financial statements.

Example Calculation:

- ◦ **Trial Balance**: Prepared from the ledger to ensure that total debits equal total credits.

  - ▪ **Total Debits**: $50,000
  - ▪ **Total Credits**: $50,000

A balanced trial balance indicates that the ledger entries are accurate and complete.

2. Preparation of Financial Statements

The information from the ledger is used to prepare financial statements, including the balance sheet, income statement, and cash flow statement. The general ledger provides the necessary data for these statements, ensuring that they reflect the company's financial position and performance accurately.

Bollywood Parallel: *Lagaan*

In *Lagaan*, the culmination of the cricket match determines the outcome of the entire story. Similarly, the ledger's detailed records culminate in the preparation of financial statements, which present the company's financial results and position.

Example Calculation:

- ◦ **Balance Sheet**: Prepared using data from the general ledger.

  - ▪ **Assets**: $100,000
  - ▪ **Liabilities**: $60,000
  - ▪ **Equity**: $40,000

- ○ **Income Statement**: Prepared using revenue and expense data from the general ledger.

  - ▪ **Revenue**: $80,000
  - ▪ **Expenses**: $50,000
  - ▪ **Net Income**: $30,000

These statements provide a comprehensive view of the company's financial health and performance.

Bollywood Dialogue: "Picture abhi baaki hai mere dost" (*Om Shanti Om*)

This iconic dialogue translates to "The movie is not over yet, my friend," emphasizing that there is more to come. Similarly, the ledger ensures that all financial details are accounted for before the final financial statements are prepared. Just as the film reel holds all recorded scenes, the ledger holds all financial transactions, providing a complete and detailed record that is essential for accurate financial reporting.

6.4 Conclusion

The ledger is a fundamental component of the accounting system, serving as the central repository for all financial transactions. Much like the film reel captures every scene in a movie, the ledger consolidates all financial data, ensuring that every transaction is recorded and classified accurately. By maintaining detailed records through the general ledger and subsidiary ledgers, businesses can ensure the accuracy and completeness of their financial reporting.

Understanding the role of the ledger in the accounting process is crucial for preparing reliable financial statements and maintaining financial integrity. Just as every scene in a film contributes to the overall narrative, every transaction recorded in the ledger contributes to the company's financial story, ensuring that the final financial statements reflect a true and fair view of the company's financial position and performance.

6.5 Summary

1. **Introduction**: The ledger is the central record of all financial transactions, essential for accurate financial reporting.
2. **The Ledger:**

   - **General Ledger**: Contains all accounts needed for financial statements, including assets, liabilities, equity, revenues, and expenses.
   - **Subsidiary Ledgers**: Provide detailed records for specific areas like accounts receivable and payable.

3. **Role in Financial Reporting:**

   - **Accuracy and Reconciliation**: Ensures transactions are accurately recorded and reconciled.
   - **Preparation of Financial Statements**: Data from the ledger is used to create balance sheets, income statements, and cash flow statements.

4. **Conclusion**: The ledger ensures every financial transaction is recorded, contributing to reliable financial statements.

CHAPTER SEVEN

Editing – Adjusting Entries

7.1 Introduction

"Teja main hoon, mark idhar hai." – Andaz Apna Apna

Adjusting entries are like the final edits in a movie. Before the financial statements are ready for release, adjustments are made to ensure everything is perfect. *"Galtiyon ko theek karna zaroori hai, kyunki Teja main hoon, mark idhar hai!"* These adjustments make sure that revenue and expenses are recorded in the right period.

In filmmaking, editing is a crucial stage where raw footage is refined and polished to ensure continuity and coherence. This process helps to craft a seamless narrative that aligns with the vision of the director and the script. Similarly, in accounting, adjusting entries are essential for refining financial records to present an accurate and fair depiction of a company's financial position. These entries adjust the accounts to reflect the true economic events and conditions of a company as of the financial reporting date. This chapter explores the importance of adjusting entries in accounting, drawing parallels with the editing process in filmmaking to illustrate their role in achieving financial accuracy.

7.2 Adjusting Entries

Definition

Adjusting entries are journal entries made at the end of an accounting period to update the accounts before preparing financial statements. These entries ensure that the financial statements accurately reflect the company's financial position and performance by accounting for revenues and expenses in the period in which they occur. Adjusting entries are necessary because certain transactions are not recorded or fully accounted for during the normal course of business, requiring adjustments to align with accrual accounting principles.

Examples

1. Accrued Expenses

Definition: Accrued expenses are costs that have been incurred but not yet paid or recorded. These expenses are recognized in the accounting period in which they occur, even if payment will be made in a future period.

Example: Consider a company that has received utility services in December but will not receive the bill until January. The expense for these services needs to be recorded in December to reflect the accurate cost for that period.

Bollywood Parallel: *Kabhi Khushi Kabhie Gham*

Just as *Kabhi Khushi Kabhie Gham* showcases the complex relationships and unresolved issues among family members that need to be addressed for the story to unfold properly, accrued expenses address the costs that have been incurred but not yet documented in the financial records, ensuring the story of financial performance is complete.

Journal Entry Example:

- ◦ **Expense Account (Utilities Expense):** Debit $1,000
- ◦ **Liability Account (Utilities Payable):** Credit $1,000

This entry records the expense that has been incurred but not yet paid, ensuring that the financial statements reflect the true cost for the period.

1. Depreciation

Definition: Depreciation is the allocation of the cost of a fixed asset over its useful life. This accounting method spreads the expense of an asset over the periods in which it is used, matching the cost with the revenues it helps to generate.

Example: If a company purchases equipment for $10,000 with a useful life of 5 years, it should record depreciation expense annually to reflect the asset's consumption over time.

Bollywood Parallel: *Zindagi Na Milegi Dobara*

In *Zindagi Na Milegi Dobara*, the film explores the journey of the characters over time, showing how their experiences and relationships evolve. Similarly, depreciation spreads the cost of an asset over its useful life, reflecting its gradual wear and tear as it contributes to the company's operations over time.

Journal Entry Example:

- ○ **Expense Account (Depreciation Expense)**: Debit $2,000
- ○ **Contra-Asset Account (Accumulated Depreciation)**: Credit $2,000

This entry records the depreciation expense for the period, reducing the asset's book value to reflect its usage and wear.

3. **Prepaid Expenses**

Definition: Prepaid expenses are costs paid in advance for services or goods that will be used or received in future periods. These expenses need to be allocated over the periods they benefit.

Example: If a company pays $12,000 for a one-year insurance policy in advance, the expense should be allocated over the 12 months, rather than being recognized in full in the month of payment.

Bollywood Parallel: *Dil Chahta Hai*

Much like *Dil Chahta Hai* portrays the different phases of life and how the characters' experiences unfold over time, prepaid expenses are spread out over multiple periods, aligning the expense recognition with the benefit received from the prepaid services or goods.

Journal Entry Example:

- ○ **Initial Payment:**

  - ▪ **Asset Account (Prepaid Insurance)**: Debit $12,000
  - ▪ **Cash Account**: Credit $12,000

- ○ **Monthly Adjustment:**

    - ▪ **Expense Account (Insurance Expense):** Debit $1,000
    - ▪ **Asset Account (Prepaid Insurance):** Credit $1,000

This entry records the monthly allocation of the prepaid insurance cost, reflecting the expense in the periods it covers.

7.3 Importance of Adjusting Entries

1. **Ensuring Accurate Financial Reporting**

Adjusting entries are essential for ensuring that the financial statements accurately reflect the company's financial performance and position. Without these adjustments, financial statements may misrepresent the company's true economic situation, leading to incorrect conclusions and decisions.

Bollywood Parallel: *Om Shanti Om*

Just as *Om Shanti Om* requires precise editing to ensure the story flows seamlessly and all plot points are resolved, adjusting entries refine the financial records to present a complete and accurate financial picture, ensuring that all revenues and expenses are properly accounted for.

Example:

- ○ **Adjusted Trial Balance:** Prepared after making adjusting entries to ensure that total debits equal total credits, and the financial statements accurately reflect the company's financial status.

2. Aligning with Accrual Accounting Principles

Adjusting entries align financial reporting with accrual accounting principles, which require revenues and expenses to be recognized in the periods in which they occur, regardless of when cash transactions happen. This approach provides a more accurate representation of a company's financial performance.

Bollywood Parallel: *Lagaan*

In *Lagaan*, the accurate portrayal of events and characters is crucial for the story's impact. Similarly, adjusting entries ensure that financial reports align with accrual accounting principles, providing a true and fair view of the company's financial activities.

Example:

- **Accrued Revenue**: Recognizing revenue earned but not yet billed or received in cash, ensuring that financial statements reflect the true performance of the company for the period.

Bollywood Dialogue: "Har ek friend zaroori hota hai" (*Friends*)

This dialogue translates to "Every friend is important," highlighting the significance of each individual in completing a storyline. Similarly, adjusting entries are crucial in completing the financial picture, ensuring that every aspect of financial performance is accurately recorded and reflected in the financial statements. Just as each friend plays a pivotal role in the narrative, each adjusting entry plays a vital role in ensuring the financial statements are complete and accurate.

7.4 Conclusion

Adjusting entries are a vital part of the accounting process, much like editing is essential in filmmaking. They refine financial records to accurately reflect the company's financial position and performance by updating accounts to align with accrual accounting principles. By addressing accrued expenses, depreciation, and prepaid expenses, adjusting entries ensure that the financial statements present a true and fair view of the company's financial activities. Understanding the role of adjusting entries helps in preparing accurate financial reports, providing valuable insights into the company's financial health and performance. Just as editing brings together all elements of a film to create a cohesive narrative, adjusting entries bring together all financial data to present a complete and accurate financial picture.

7.5 Summary

1. **Introduction**: Adjusting entries are like final edits in a movie, ensuring financial statements reflect accurate revenue and expenses.

2. **Adjusting Entries:**

   - **Accrued Expenses**: Costs incurred but not yet paid; recorded in the correct period.
   - **Depreciation**: Spreads asset cost over its useful life.

- ◦ **Prepaid Expenses**: Costs paid in advance, allocated over time.

3. **Importance**:

   - ◦ **Accurate Financial Reporting**: Ensures financial statements are precise.
   - ◦ **Aligning with Accrual Accounting**: Reflects true economic events, matching revenues and expenses to the correct period.

4. **Conclusion**: Adjusting entries refine financial data for accurate and fair reporting, similar to how editing perfects a film's narrative.

The Premiere – Financial Statements

8.1 Introduction

"Kaun kambakht bardaasht karne ke liye peeta hai?" – Devdas

The financial statements are the grand premiere – the moment of truth. *"Kaun kambakht profit dekhne ke liye financial statement banata hai?"* Investors, creditors, and stakeholders all look at these statements to judge the company's performance, just like an audience watches a movie's premiere to see how it turned out.

In filmmaking, the premiere is the grand event where the film is finally revealed to the audience. It's the culmination of months of meticulous work—scriptwriting, directing, acting, and editing—all coming together to showcase the final product. Similarly, in accounting, the financial statements are the culmination of a company's financial activities over a period. They present a comprehensive overview of the company's financial performance and position, summarizing the results of all accounting activities. This chapter explores the four primary financial statements—the Balance Sheet, Income

Statement, Cash Flow Statement, and Statement of Retained Earnings—detailing their roles and significance in portraying the company's financial story.

8.2 Financial Statements

Definition

Financial statements are formal records that provide a summary of a company's financial performance and position. They are prepared at the end of an accounting period and include:

- **Balance Sheet**: Shows the company's assets, liabilities, and equity at a specific point in time.
- **Balance Sheet**: *"Yeh toh picture ka interval hai, abhi climax baaki hai!"* It shows the company's financial position at a specific moment.
- **Income Statement**: Details the company's revenues, expenses, and profits or losses over a period.
- **Income Statement**: *"Hum profit aur loss ke beech ka fark samajhte hain."* This statement shows how much the company earned and spent during the period.
- **Cash Flow Statement**: Provides information on cash inflows and outflows from operating, investing, and financing activities.
- **Cash Flow Statement**: *"Paisa bolta hai, aur yeh statement batata hai paisa kahan se aaya aur kahan gaya!"*
- **Statement of Retained Earnings**: Shows changes in equity, specifically how profits are retained or distributed over time.

These statements collectively offer a snapshot of the company's financial health, guiding stakeholders such as investors, creditors, and management in making informed decisions.

Examples

1. Balance Sheet

Definition: The Balance Sheet, also known as the Statement of Financial Position, presents a snapshot of a company's assets, liabilities, and equity as of a specific date. It is based on the fundamental accounting equation:

Assets = Liabilities + Equity

Example: Consider a company's balance sheet at year-end showing:

- **Assets**: Cash ($50,000), Inventory ($30,000), Equipment ($100,000)
- **Liabilities**: Accounts Payable ($20,000), Long-term Debt ($60,000)
- **Equity**: Common Stock ($80,000), Retained Earnings ($20,000)

Bollywood Parallel: *Kabhi Khushi Kabhie Gham*

Just as *Kabhi Khushi Kabhie Gham* presents a detailed view of the complex family dynamics and relationships at a specific point in time, the Balance Sheet provides a detailed snapshot of the company's financial position at a particular date. It reveals how resources are distributed and financed, offering insights into the company's financial stability and structure.

Significance: The Balance Sheet helps stakeholders assess the company's liquidity (ability to meet short-term obligations), solvency (ability to meet long-term obligations), and overall financial stability.

1. Income Statement

Definition: The Income Statement, also known as the Profit and Loss Statement, summarizes the company's revenues, expenses, and profits or losses over a specific period. It shows how well the company performs financially during that time frame.

Example: An Income Statement for a quarter might show:

- **Revenue**: Sales ($200,000)
- **Expenses**: Cost of Goods Sold ($120,000), Operating Expenses ($40,000)
- **Net Profit**: $40,000

Bollywood Parallel: *Chakde! India*

Similar to how *Chakde! India* captures the highs and lows of the hockey team's journey throughout the tournament, the Income Statement reflects the company's financial performance over a period. It provides a narrative of how revenue is earned and expenses are incurred, ultimately revealing the company's profitability.

Significance: The Income Statement helps stakeholders evaluate the company's operational efficiency, profitability, and overall performance.

3. Cash Flow Statement

Definition: The Cash Flow Statement provides a detailed account of the company's cash inflows and outflows from operating, investing, and financing activities during a period. It is crucial for understanding how the company generates and uses cash.

Example: A Cash Flow Statement might include:

- ○ **Operating Activities**: Cash received from customers ($180,000), Cash paid to suppliers ($100,000)
- ○ **Investing Activities**: Purchase of Equipment ($30,000)
- ○ **Financing Activities**: Proceeds from Loan ($20,000), Dividends Paid ($10,000)

Bollywood Parallel: *Dil Chahta Hai*

Just as *Dil Chahta Hai* shows how the friends navigate through different phases of life and their evolving relationships, the Cash Flow Statement illustrates the company's cash movements and how they impact the overall financial health. It provides insights into the company's liquidity and ability to sustain operations, invest in growth, and return value to shareholders.

Significance: The Cash Flow Statement helps stakeholders assess the company's cash management, liquidity, and ability to fund operations and investments.

4. Statement of Retained Earnings

Definition: The Statement of Retained Earnings details the changes in equity, specifically how much of the company's profit is retained for future use versus distributed to shareholders as dividends. It reconciles the beginning and ending retained earnings for a period.

Example: A Statement of Retained Earnings might show:

- ○ **Beginning Retained Earnings**: $10,000
- ○ **Add: Net Profit**: $30,000

- ◦ **Less: Dividends Paid**: $5,000
- ◦ **Ending Retained Earnings**: $35,000

Bollywood Parallel: *Lagaan*

Just as *Lagaan* follows the story of villagers investing their time and efforts into overcoming challenges for future prosperity, the Statement of Retained Earnings tracks how profits are reinvested into the company or distributed to shareholders. It shows the long-term impact of financial decisions on the company's equity.

Significance: The Statement of Retained Earnings provides insights into how profits are utilized, reflecting the company's growth strategy and its approach to rewarding shareholders.

Bollywood Dialogue: "Dil se jo baat nikalti hai" (*Rang De Basanti***)**

This dialogue, which translates to "What comes from the heart," reflects the deep emotions and sincerity behind a message. Similarly, financial statements reflect the true financial state of the company, providing a transparent and heartfelt view of its financial performance and position. They encapsulate the essence of the company's financial activities, offering stakeholders a genuine insight into its economic reality.

8.3 Conclusion

The premiere of a film reveals the culmination of creative and technical efforts, presenting the final product to the audience. In accounting, financial statements serve a similar purpose, presenting the culmination of a company's financial activities and providing a comprehensive view of its financial performance and position. The Balance Sheet,

Income Statement, Cash Flow Statement, and Statement of Retained Earnings each play a crucial role in telling the company's financial story. They collectively offer a detailed snapshot of the company's economic reality, helping stakeholders make informed decisions. Understanding these financial statements is essential for interpreting the company's financial health and making strategic decisions, just as understanding a film's plot and characters is crucial for appreciating its story and impact.

8.4 Summary

1. **Introduction**: Financial statements are like a film's premiere, showcasing the company's performance for stakeholders to judge.
2. **Financial Statements**:

   - **Balance Sheet**: Shows the company's financial position (assets, liabilities, equity) at a specific date.
   - **Income Statement**: Summarizes revenues, expenses, and profits/losses over a period, reflecting the company's performance.
   - **Cash Flow Statement**: Details cash inflows and outflows from operating, investing, and financing activities.
   - **Statement of Retained Earnings**: Shows changes in equity, focusing on profits retained or distributed.

3. **Conclusion**: Financial statements, like a film premiere, present the culmination of a company's financial activities, helping stakeholders make informed decisions.

CHAPTER NINE

The Reviews - Audits

9.1 Introduction

"Mere Karan Arjun aayenge." – Karan Arjun

Just like Karan Arjun came back to seek justice, auditors come to review the financial statements and ensure they're accurate. "Yeh audit tumhare statements ko sachai ki kasauti par kasne aaya hai!" A clean audit report is like a five-star review for a blockbuster hit – it boosts the company's credibility and trustworthiness.

In filmmaking, reviews are crucial to ensure that the final product meets quality standards and adheres to industry norms. Just as film critics and audiences evaluate a film's success based on various criteria, audits play a similar role in the world of accounting. Audits assess the accuracy, completeness, and compliance of financial statements with accounting principles and regulations. They serve as a critical review mechanism, ensuring that financial reports provide a true and fair view of a company's financial performance and position. This chapter delves into the concept of audits, exploring their types, purposes, and significance in maintaining financial integrity and transparency.

9.2 Audits

Definition

An audit is an independent examination of financial statements and related financial information to ensure accuracy and compliance with applicable accounting standards and regulations. Audits are conducted to provide assurance to stakeholders that the financial statements are free from material misstatement and present a true and fair view of the company's financial position.

Types of Audits

1. External Audits

Definition: External audits are performed by independent auditors who are not part of the company's internal team. These auditors assess the financial statements to provide an objective opinion on their accuracy and adherence to generally accepted accounting principles (GAAP) or international financial reporting standards (IFRS).

Purpose: The primary purpose of an external audit is to provide assurance to external stakeholders, such as investors, creditors, and regulators, that the financial statements are reliable and trustworthy.

Example: Suppose a publicly traded company undergoes an external audit at the end of its fiscal year. The external auditors review the company's financial records, test transactions, and assess internal controls. Their audit report might state, "In our opinion, the financial statements present a true and fair view of the company's financial position as of December 31, 2023, in accordance with

GAAP."

Bollywood Parallel: *Chakde! India*

Just as *Chakde! India* showcases the intense scrutiny and evaluation of the hockey team's performance by the national selectors and coaches, external audits involve rigorous examination by independent auditors to ensure the accuracy and fairness of financial statements. The external audit provides stakeholders with confidence in the company's financial reports, akin to how a thorough review boosts the team's credibility and chances of success.

Significance: External audits enhance the credibility of financial statements and provide stakeholders with confidence in the company's financial reporting. They help detect errors, fraud, and non-compliance, ensuring that the company adheres to accounting standards and regulatory requirements.

1. Internal Audits

Definition: Internal audits are conducted by the company's own internal audit team. These audits focus on evaluating the effectiveness of internal controls, risk management processes, and operational efficiency.

Purpose: The primary purpose of internal audits is to help the company improve its operations, ensure compliance with internal policies and procedures, and identify areas for improvement.

Example: An internal audit team within a company might conduct a review of its procurement process to ensure that it adheres to company policies and effectively manages supplier relationships. The internal audit report might highlight areas where controls can be strengthened or processes can be optimized.

Bollywood Parallel: *3 Idiots*

Similar to how *3 Idiots* explores the internal dynamics of a college, revealing the strengths and weaknesses of the education system, internal audits delve into the company's internal processes and controls. They assess the efficiency and effectiveness of operations, helping the company to enhance its internal practices and achieve its objectives.

Significance: Internal audits help companies maintain effective internal controls, mitigate risks, and improve operational efficiency. They provide valuable insights and recommendations for enhancing processes and ensuring that the company operates within its established policies and procedures.

9.3 The Auditing Process

The auditing process involves several key steps to ensure a thorough and accurate review:

1. **Planning:** Auditors develop an audit plan based on an understanding of the company's operations, risks, and internal controls. This involves setting audit objectives, determining the scope of the audit, and identifying areas of focus.

2. **Fieldwork:** Auditors perform detailed testing and examination of financial transactions, records, and internal controls. This includes reviewing documentation, conducting interviews, and performing analytical procedures.

3. **Reporting:** Auditors compile their findings and prepare an audit report. The report includes the auditor's opinion on the financial statements, any identified issues or deficiencies, and recommendations for

improvement.

4. **Follow-Up:** In some cases, auditors may perform follow-up procedures to ensure that the company has addressed any issues or recommendations identified in the audit report.

Bollywood Dialogue: "Tumhare paas kya hai?" (*Bajrangi Bhaijaan*)

This dialogue, translating to "What do you have?" reflects the importance of verifying and understanding what is truly present. Similarly, audits are conducted to verify the accuracy and completeness of financial statements, ensuring that stakeholders have a clear and accurate view of the company's financial status. Just as the characters in *Bajrangi Bhaijaan* seek to uncover the truth about each other's intentions and circumstances, audits uncover the true financial state of the company, providing assurance and transparency.

9.4 Conclusion

Audits play a crucial role in the financial reporting ecosystem, serving as a comprehensive review mechanism to ensure accuracy, compliance, and transparency. External audits provide independent assurance to stakeholders about the reliability of financial statements, while internal audits focus on enhancing internal controls and operational efficiency. The auditing process involves meticulous planning, fieldwork, reporting, and follow-up to ensure a thorough evaluation. By uncovering the true financial state of the company, audits help build trust with stakeholders and support informed decision-making. Just as reviews and critiques are vital to the success of a film, audits are essential for maintaining financial integrity and fostering confidence in financial reporting.

9.5 Summary

1. **Introduction**: Audits are like reviews for a film, ensuring financial statements are accurate and reliable.
2. **Types of Audits**:

   - **External Audits**: Conducted by independent auditors to verify accuracy and compliance for external stakeholders.
   - **Internal Audits**: Performed by the company's internal team to evaluate controls, risk management, and operational efficiency.

3. **Auditing Process**:

   - **Planning**: Setting objectives and scope.
   - **Fieldwork**: Testing transactions and internal controls.
   - **Reporting**: Preparing an audit report with findings and recommendations.
   - **Follow-Up**: Ensuring issues are addressed.

4. **Conclusion**: Audits ensure financial integrity and transparency, building trust and supporting informed decision-making.

The Cinematic And Financial Narrative

In both Bollywood and accounting, every component plays a crucial role in creating a coherent and compelling story. Bollywood, with its intricate blend of script, direction, acting, and reviews, parallels the way accounting integrates principles, transactions, ledgers, adjustments, financial statements, and audits to present a business's financial narrative.

In filmmaking, the script provides the foundational blueprint, similar to how accounting principles like GAAP and IFRS guide financial reporting. Just as a director ensures that each scene aligns with the script, accountants ensure financial transactions are accurately recorded and reported. The cast in a film—comprising assets, liabilities, and equity—drives the financial story, just as characters drive the plot of a movie.

The Accounting Equation acts as the plot, maintaining balance and coherence in financial reporting. Each financial transaction impacts the overall narrative, much like scenes in a film shape the story. The Ledger holds all financial records in sequence, akin to a film reel preserving the entire movie.

Adjusting Entries refine financial records to ensure accuracy, paralleling how editing improves a film's continuity. Financial Statements reveal the culmination of accounting efforts, similar to how a film premiere showcases the final product. Finally, Audits review and verify financial statements, much like film reviews assess a movie's quality and adherence to standards.

Understanding these accounting concepts through Bollywood analogies enriches our appreciation of the artistry and precision involved in both fields. Whether crafting a cinematic masterpiece or ensuring financial integrity, the goal is to present a compelling and transparent narrative that resonates with its audience.

www.ingramcontent.com/pod-product-compliance
Lightning Source LLC
Chambersburg PA
CBHW021122130726

47988CB00003B/1122